Contents

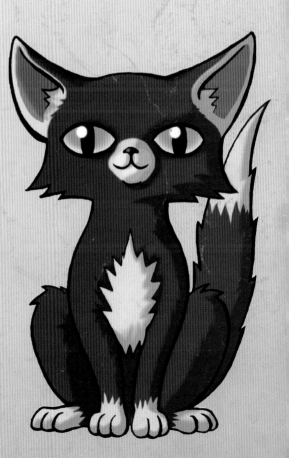

Introduction

Manga now features in a huge range of magazines, computer games and graphic novels. It is one of the most visible drawing styles in the world today, and one of the most popular among comic-book fans.

Although the main characters of manga comics and animes (the Japanese word for animations) are usually human, they are often supported by a cast of animals, from cuddly little four-legged sidekicks to enormous dinosaurs. It's these weird and wonderful creatures that we'll be focusing on in this book.

In *How to Draw Manga Animals* you'll find a wealth of exercises to get you started on drawing in the manga style. There are easy-to-follow steps for you to create a range of characters, and you'll also find examples to help you develop your own cast of amazing creatures.

The most important skill for any aspiring manga artist to develop is the ability to draw, and this will only come about if you keep practising. All this effort will pay off eventually, and you will notice how much more inventive and interesting your drawings become.

Kitsu

Kitsu is a resourceful young fox who moved into the big city in search of action and adventure. Life on the streets is tough and he needs to keep his wits about him constantly. Any chance he gets, he sneaks into movie theatres and sniffs out discarded comics in trash cans, so he's spent a lot of time looking at manga. Kitsu will be popping up from time to time to help you in your quest for manga mastery. He may only be a fox, but he's got a keen eye and knows what he's talking about.

Materials

Pencils are graded H, HB or B according to their hardness. H pencils are the hardest. These pencils will make lighter lines. B pencils are softer and will make darker lines. Most general-purpose pencils found at home or school are graded HB. For the exercises in this book, it will help you to use a hard pencil, like an H, for sketching light guidelines and a soft pencil for making the final lines of each of your drawings distinct. Get an HB mechanical pencil if at all possible, since this will produce a constant fine line for your final image. If your pencils aren't mechanical, they'll need sharpening regularly.

You'll need an eraser too, since you'll have to sketch a lot of rough lines to get your drawing right and you'll want to get rid of those lines once you have a drawing you're happy with. Keep your eraser as clean as possible.

When it comes to colouring, coloured pencils are easiest to use. You might want to start with them and then move on to felt-tip pens and watercolour paints when you have developed your skills further. Cheap photocopier paper was used for most of the artworks in this book, and it's quite adequate for most types of drawing. Only if you're working with paints should you purchase thicker paper since it won't tear or buckle when it gets wet.

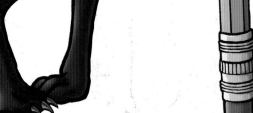

Cute Creatures

For manga artwork aimed at younger children, cutesy cartoon-style characters are very common. Even in stories aimed at older audiences, cute animals often feature as stooges to the main characters, or provide some light relief from the violence of a fight scene.

Whatever kind of creature you want to draw, the principles are the same. You start with a set of simple geometric shapes that form the main body masses, then work on the smaller details.

Cute Cat – Front View

You could probably do a good job of drawing this cute cat just by copying the final picture. But if you learn to construct it one step at a time, this will help you when you draw more complicated characters and viewpoints.

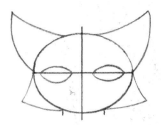

Step 1
Take a hard pencil and use light lines to draw an oval for the head. To help you make your picture symmetrical, put a vertical and a horizontal line through the centre of it. For the eyes, draw two ovals with pointed ends. The ears and long fur around the face can be drawn as rough triangle shapes.

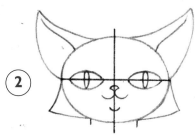

Step 2
Adding a few more simple lines will complete the facial features.

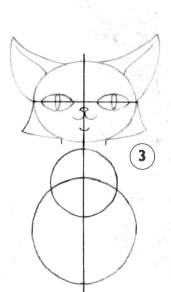

Step 3
Extend the vertical guideline to help you draw the body. Two overlapping circles make its basic shape.

Step 4
The smaller circle will help you draw the slender chest and front legs. The bigger circle will help you position the back legs. The tail sits upright.

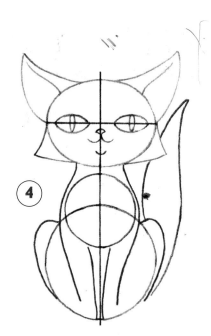

Step 5

Add some jagged lines to create the texture of the fur. Longer strokes will make a fluffier cat and shorter strokes will make the coat smoother. Add the paws.

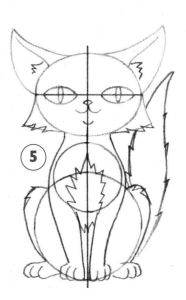

Step 6

Use a soft pencil to make the good lines of your drawing heavier. Erase your rough lines as you go along. Shade in the pupils, but leave a circle of white in the top left of each eye to form the bright highlights. Go over your final lines again with a black felt-tip pen. When the ink is dry, erase any remaining pencil marks.

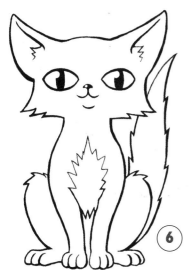

Step 7

This is what your finished drawing should look like. Try colouring your cat with pencils, paints or felt-tips.

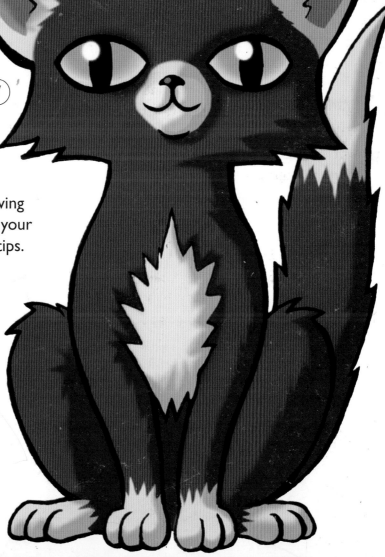

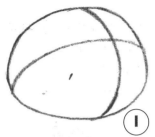

Cute Cat – Side View

Here our cute cat has turned his body to the side. His head, however, is turned only half way between the front and side, so it is at a 3/4 angle.

Step 1
Draw an oval shape for the head, but make it more squashed than the one you drew for the front view. The change of viewpoint also means that the vertical and horizontal guidelines now curve to follow the rounded shape of the head as shown.

Step 2
Use your guidelines to help you place the facial features as shown. Notice that the eye to the right of your picture is drawn smaller because it is turned further away. The ear on that side is smaller too.

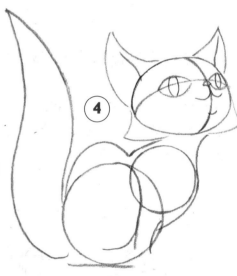

Step 3
Draw two overlapping circles to help you form the shape of the body. Study the picture to copy the size and positioning of the circles.

Step 4
Add the cat's body outline using your circles to guide you. Make the upright tail long and curved.

Step 5
Add some jagged lines to show the texture of the fur. Shape the paws and add a circle to each eye for the bright highlights. The circle on the eye to the right of your picture will be smaller than the one to the left.

Step 6

Use a soft pencil to go over the lines that you want to form your final drawing. Erase your rough lines as you go. Shade the pupils of the eyes black, leaving the bright highlights white. Next, go over your drawing again using a black felt-tip pen. When the ink dries, erase any remaining pencil lines, including the framework for the head and the circles that formed the body shape.

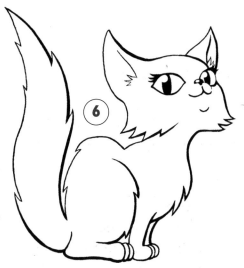

Step 7

The great thing about manga creatures is that they can be whatever colour you choose. Colour your cat as you did before or try using a different colour scheme.

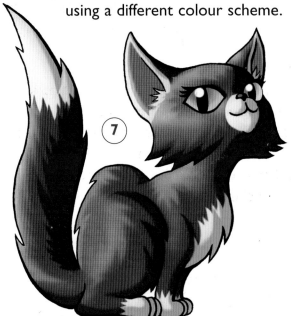

Cute Proportions

In manga, as with all styles of drawing, characters are measured in head heights. This refers to the size of the character's body in relation to its own head. Changing the body's proportions can have a big effect.

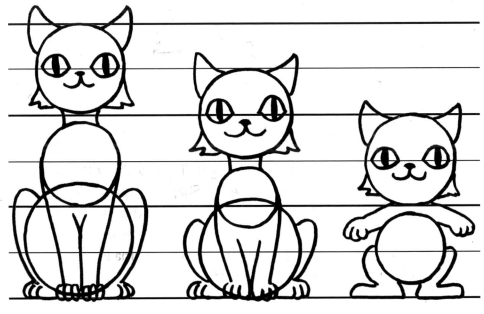

3 heads tall   **2¹/₂ heads tall**   **2 heads tall**

The cute cat featured in the previous two exercises is about two-and-a-half heads tall, which is fairly standard for characters of this type. Three heads and two heads tall are also quite common. Remember that the smaller the body is in relation to the head, the younger and cuter the character will look.

Study the pictures (left) to see how the body shape has been changed by using different-sized circles. Try drawing the cat you drew before but make him shorter or taller.

Cat Varieties

Artists can draw many variations of one animal. Here are a few of the different ways that a cat can be interpreted, depending on the style of manga drawing.

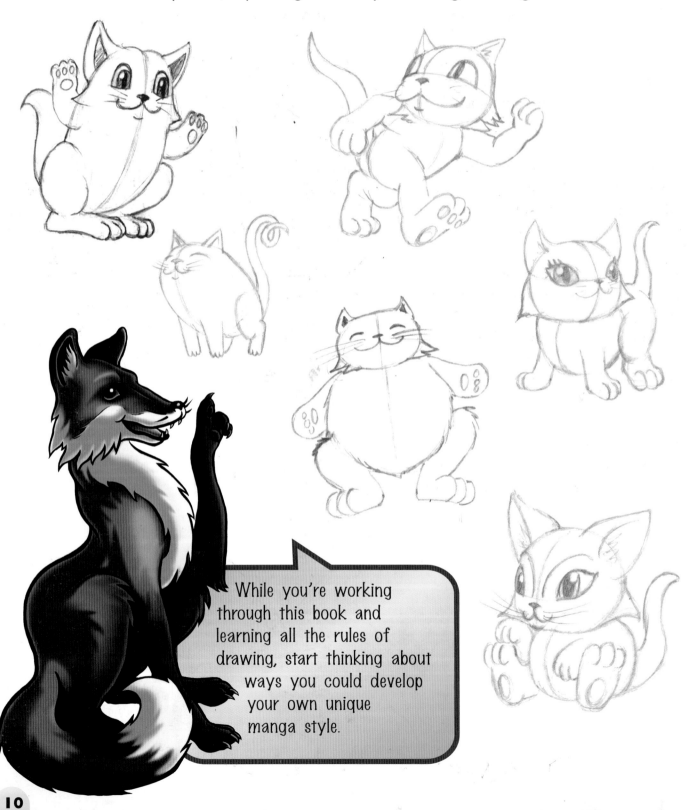

While you're working through this book and learning all the rules of drawing, start thinking about ways you could develop your own unique manga style.

Transformations

If you have a good understanding of how to draw a cute cat, it's easy to work out how you can change its personality, or even turn it into a different animal altogether. The principles are exactly the same – just a few of the details differ.

1 This is a 3/4 view of our cat, but here he's been made a little more rounded so he looks even cuter.

2 Notice how easy it is to turn our cute cat into a fierce enemy. Slanting the eyes and eyebrows and adding some sharp teeth and claws produces dramatic results.

3 Starting from the same body and head shapes, the cat can be turned into a mouse by changing the shape of the ears and eyes and adding two long front teeth. A long, thin tail completes the transformation, but you could also add a chunk of cheese for effect!

4 The same cat can be used to create a pig, squirrel, rabbit or dog. Try drawing each of them. Turn each one into an evil character too.

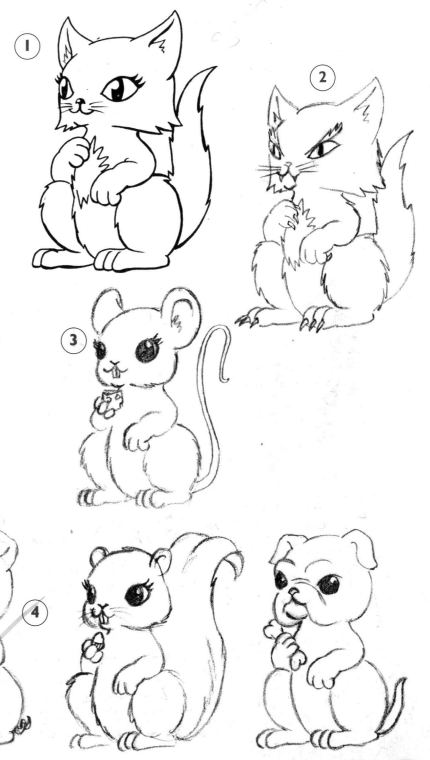

Beasts

Many animals, like deer and rabbits, are usually found in manga stories only as cute characters. For ferocious animal characters we have to look to animals that are normally associated with violence, like lions and wolves, for example.

Unlike the cute creatures, these animals are not usually drawn in a particularly stylized way, although there are, of course, some exceptions. Some manga beasts are drawn as exaggerations of real animals, with wicked-looking teeth and claws.

Lioness – 3/4 View

Here is one of the cute cat's relatives – the lioness. Imagine the head as a large ball, with a smaller ball making up the muzzle.

Step 1
Draw two overlapping circles as shown. Draw a curved vertical line on each one to mark the centre of the lioness's head. Now roughly sketch in the shape of the eyes, nose and mouth.

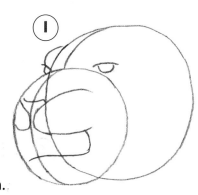

Step 2
Draw on the ears. A few more lines will shape the jawline and neck.

Step 3
Carefully copy the lines added here to make the lioness more lifelike. Notice the creases in the skin above the nose that add to her snarl, and the jagged shapes that form the fur.

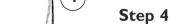

Step 4
Now for the whiskers, teeth and tongue. Take some time to get these right since they are crucial to the beast's threatening appearance.

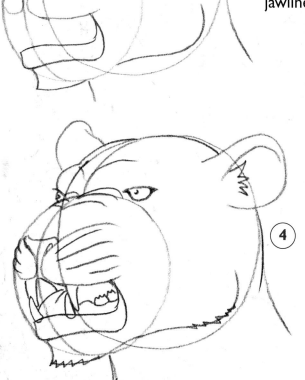

Step 5

Go over all your good lines with a soft pencil so you can clearly see the shape of your final drawing. Erase the rough lines as you go. Go over the lines again with a black felt-tip pen. The black pen has been used here to shade the nose and mouth area for effect.

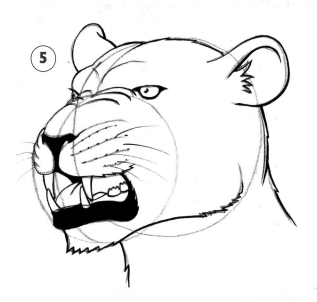

Step 6

Now you can erase the rest of your pencil guidelines, then add some colour. Copy the the way the lioness has been coloured here. Notice the different shadows on her face.

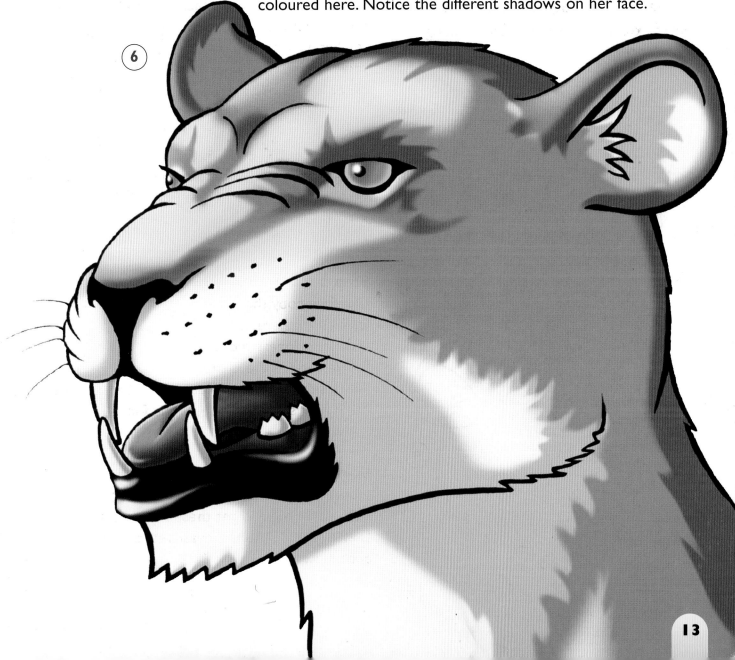

13

Fox – 3/4 View

One animal that often crops up in Japanese folklore and comics is the fox. Its head is much more angular than that of a lioness.

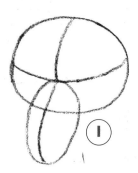

Step 1
Start with a rough oval shape for the main part of the head, then add a long narrow muzzle. Copy the curves of the vertical and horizontal guidelines. These lines will help you place all the features symmetrically.

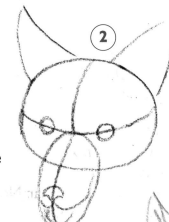

Step 2
The ears immediately make your picture identifiable as a fox. The eyes start as two small circles. Outline the nose and mouth too.

Step 3
Keep building up the features of the face. Add the loose fur to the sides of the face. Some simple scribbles form the fur inside the ears.

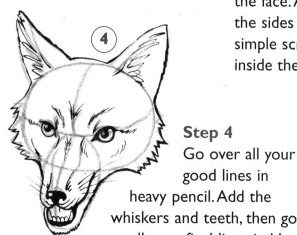

Step 4
Go over all your good lines in heavy pencil. Add the whiskers and teeth, then go over all your final lines in black ink. A few extra marks will show the texture of the fur around the eyes and at the top of the muzzle. Shade the pupils black, leaving a white circle inside each one. Use solid black on the nose and mouth too.

Step 5
Erase all your pencil marks, then add the colour. Notice how using white on the eyes adds to the fierceness of the fox's glare.

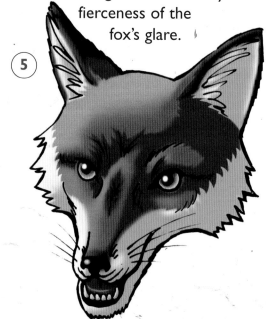

Variations

Once you've mastered drawing a fox, making a few changes to it can develop its character – or turn it into a different beast altogether.

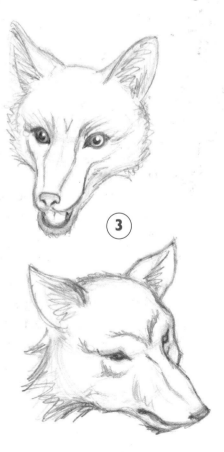

1 Evil fox
This fox is based on the same framework as the one on page 14, but it has been made to look much more evil by slanting the eyes and making the pupils smaller and the teeth longer. Sharper lines have been used for the fur.

2 Friendly fox
A friendlier fox can be created by making the eyes larger and rounder. The fur is more tufty, and curved lines make the muzzle less angular. No teeth have been drawn, so it appears that they are covered by the tongue.

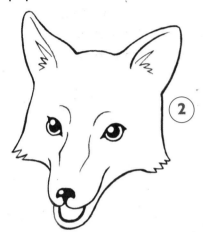

3 Fox and wolf
Here's the original fox sketch placed next to one of a wolf. You can see that they are really quite similar. To draw the wolf, break it down into the steps you followed for the fox, but look at this sketch at each stage to work out what's different. Notice that the ears sit further apart and the eyes are narrower. The muzzle is wider and the snout more pointed.

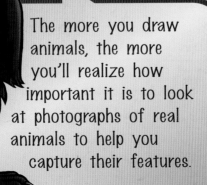

The more you draw animals, the more you'll realize how important it is to look at photographs of real animals to help you capture their features.

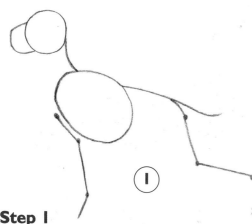

Lion Body – Side View

Let's get more ambitious and draw some complete animal bodies. We'll start with a fully grown male lion.

Step 1

Start with the head and body shapes, then add the spine and the bones of one front and one hind leg.

Step 2

Add the outline of the flesh around the bones. Carefully copy the curves as shown in the picture so you capture the lion's build. When you've drawn the line of the belly, add the second hind leg.

Step 3

Work on the rough shape of the muzzle. Add the second foreleg – you can only just see it from this angle. Draw the paws firmly placed on the ground.

Step 4

Add some curves to outline the shape of the face, mane and tail.

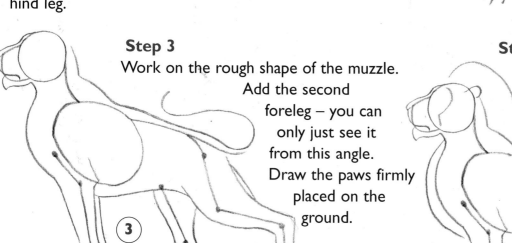

Step 5

Work on the detail of the face and add lots of little curves and curls to the mane to show that the texture is different from the smooth hair on the body. Add a tuft of fur under the chin and on the tip of the tail and a line on his belly.

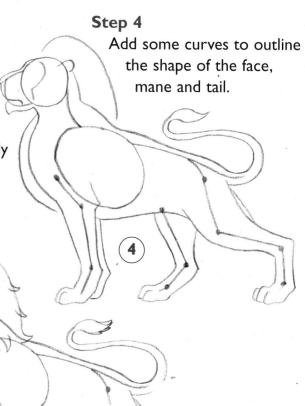

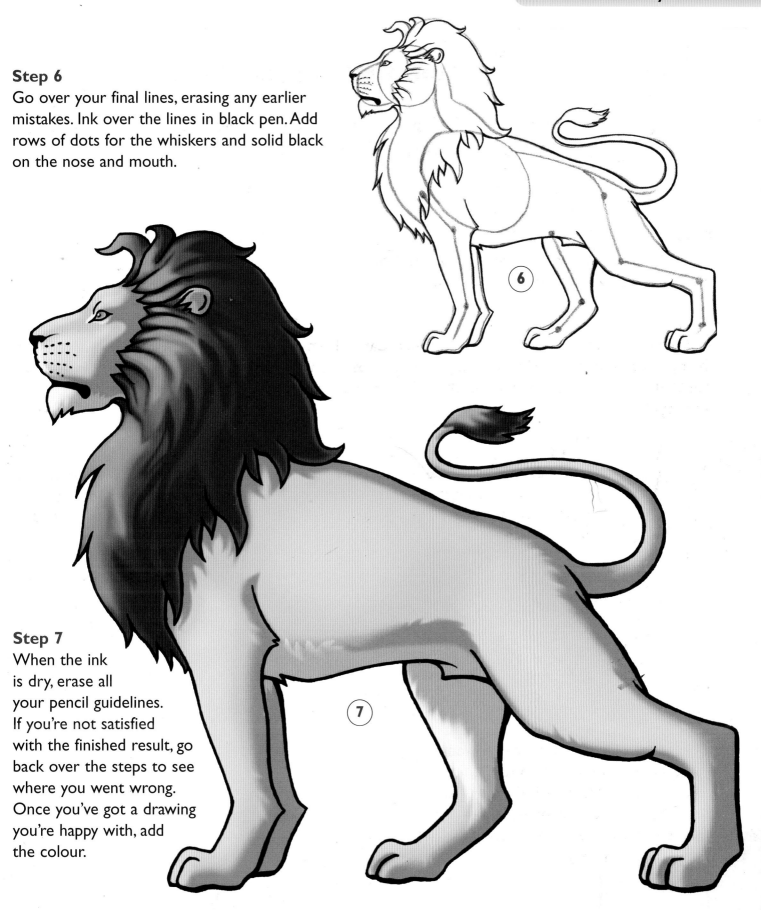

Step 6
Go over your final lines, erasing any earlier mistakes. Ink over the lines in black pen. Add rows of dots for the whiskers and solid black on the nose and mouth.

Step 7
When the ink is dry, erase all your pencil guidelines. If you're not satisfied with the finished result, go back over the steps to see where you went wrong. Once you've got a drawing you're happy with, add the colour.

Proportion Distortion

Even though the proportions of manga human characters are often highly exaggerated, those of animals seldom are. But some manga artists, influenced by Western comic styles and Hollywood animation, are beginning to give their animals a more dynamic look.

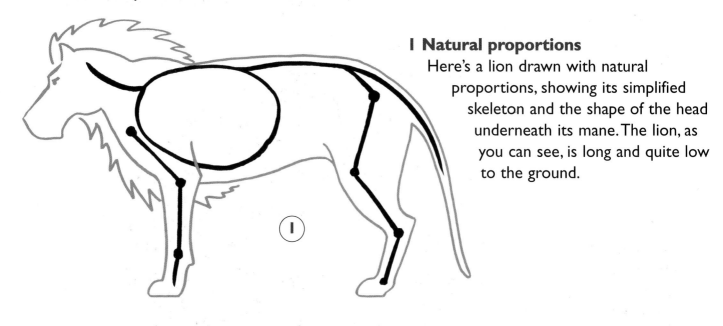

1 Natural proportions
Here's a lion drawn with natural proportions, showing its simplified skeleton and the shape of the head underneath its mane. The lion, as you can see, is long and quite low to the ground.

2 Distorted proportions
Compare this treatment of the same animal. Parts of the body have been enlarged and other parts reduced to emphasize the most powerful parts. The chest is deeper, the legs more solid, and the hindquarters have been slimmed down. The head and feet have also been enlarged to make room for huge teeth and claws.

3 Dynamic pose
Now that you've revised the proportions in a rough diagram, you can make a finished drawing of the lion in a suitably ferocious pose. The changes result in a very different-looking lion from the one on the preceding pages. This one has more dynamic proportions, a 3/4 angle of view, and an impressive display of teeth.

4 Adding colour
With the addition of colour, the transformation is complete. In line with the changes to the lion's natural form, the colour has also been exaggerated.

Animal Movement

Animals don't tend to stay still for long, especially in manga, so you need to learn to draw them in all sorts of poses, from standing and lying down to running and jumping. These pictures show some typical animal poses. The skeleton framework has been left on each body to help you see how the joints can and can't bend.

1 Lion

These two poses are typical of a lion's behaviour. Notice how different the legs look when a lion is sitting down compared with when it's stretching. Although the lion isn't in motion in either picture, the head shows that it's alert.

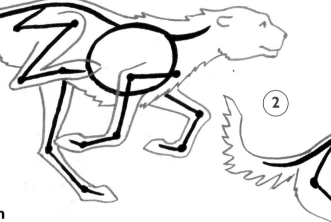

2 Cheetah

There is definitely a sense of movement in each of these drawings. The feet of the cheetah are off the ground and the head is held forward. Each picture suggests imbalance – an impression that if the animals weren't moving forward, they would fall over.

3 Horse

Even though these poses aren't balanced, the horse doesn't appear to be moving forward because it has two feet placed firmly on the ground. We still get a sense of the effort it's putting into each stance and the tension in the limbs as the horse lifts itself against the force of gravity.

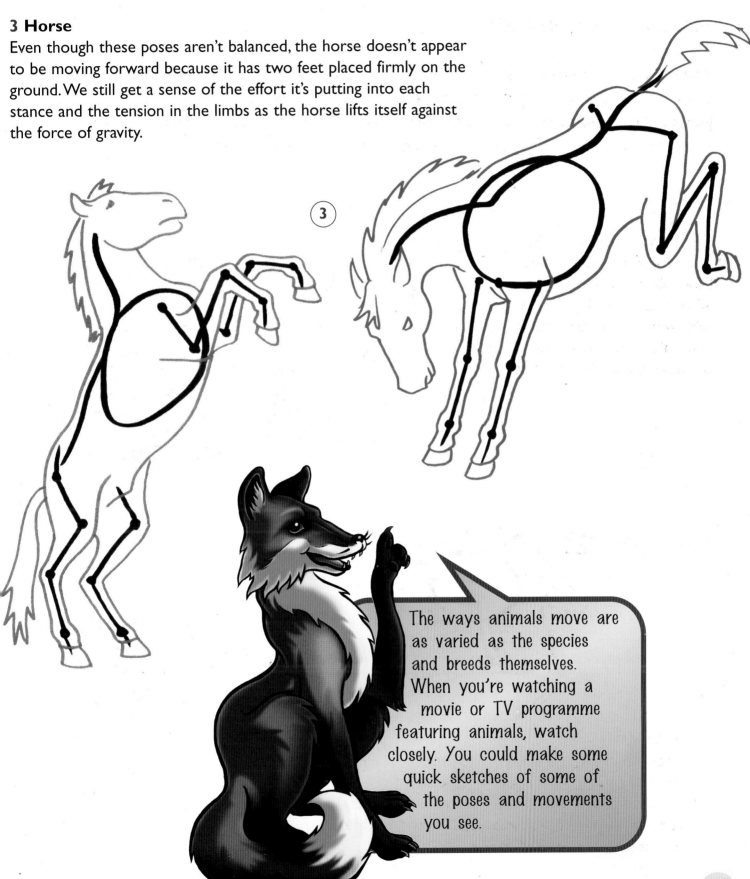

③

> The ways animals move are as varied as the species and breeds themselves. When you're watching a movie or TV programme featuring animals, watch closely. You could make some quick sketches of some of the poses and movements you see.

Wolf – Side View

These steps for drawing the body of a wolf from the side also show you how to bring movement into the pose.

Step 1

First draw the main body shapes. The muzzle should be more pointed than that of the lion and the chest takes the form of a large oval lying on its side. All but one of the legs are raised, so the bones form zigzag shapes. The tail is flying up at the back as the animal speeds along.

Step 2

Add the body outline. Where you need to create more flesh or muscle, like around the wolf's powerful hind legs, curve the line further away from the bone.

Step 3

Work on the features of the head. The ear should lie flat, the nose is high in the air and the mouth is open. Outline the feet and complete the curve of the tail.

Step 4

Lots of little jagged lines around the body outline will help show the texture of the fur. Define the paws and work on the mouth too. The tongue hangs out slightly to show that the wolf is panting.

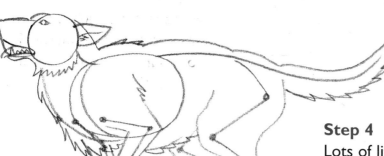

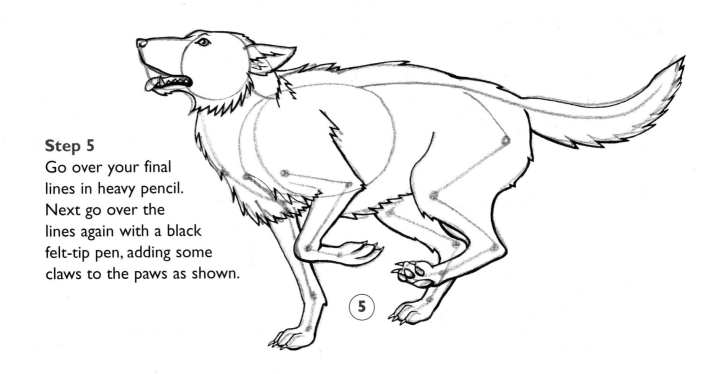

Step 5
Go over your final lines in heavy pencil. Next go over the lines again with a black felt-tip pen, adding some claws to the paws as shown.

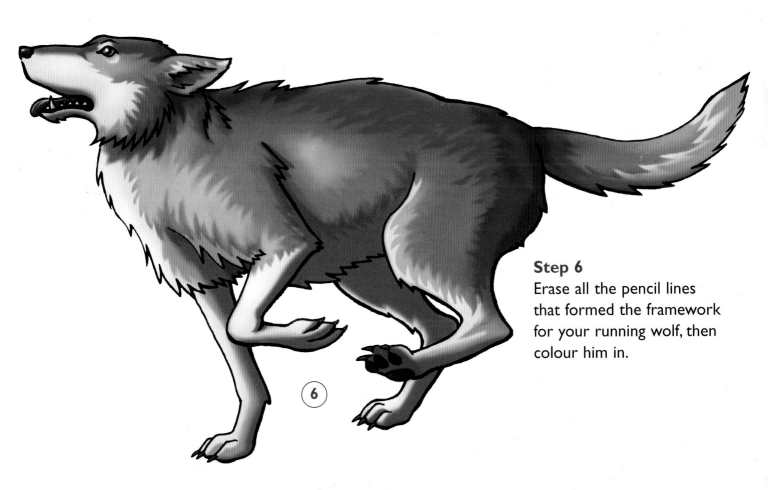

Step 6
Erase all the pencil lines that formed the framework for your running wolf, then colour him in.

Monster Dog

Turn back to pages 18–19 and you'll see how a rather ordinary-looking lion was changed into a more ferocious version. You can do this to any creature, including the wolf on the previous page. This animal can be distorted even more to create a demonic monster dog.

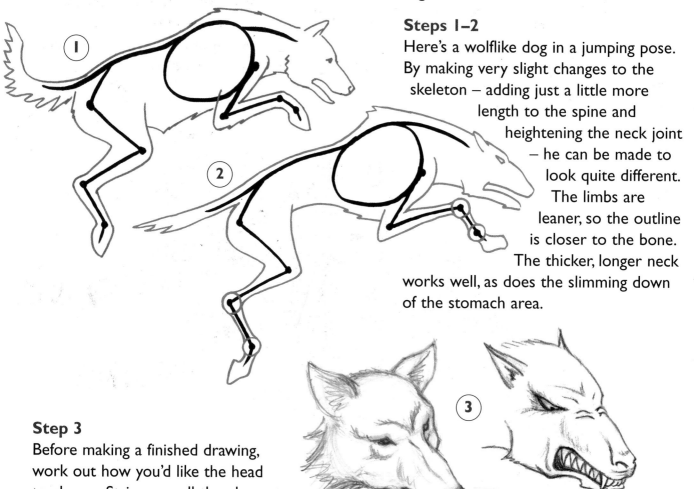

Steps 1–2
Here's a wolflike dog in a jumping pose. By making very slight changes to the skeleton – adding just a little more length to the spine and heightening the neck joint – he can be made to look quite different. The limbs are leaner, so the outline is closer to the bone. The thicker, longer neck works well, as does the slimming down of the stomach area.

Step 3
Before making a finished drawing, work out how you'd like the head to change. Strip away all the elements that could look cute. Reduce the large, soft ears to leathery spikes. Turn the friendly eyes into evil slits, and move them higher on the head. Allowing the fangs to protrude over the lips is another good trick, and a snarling expression always looks effective.

This example shows the importance of the skeleton in your drawings: if the skeleton works, then whatever alterations you make to the skin should work too.

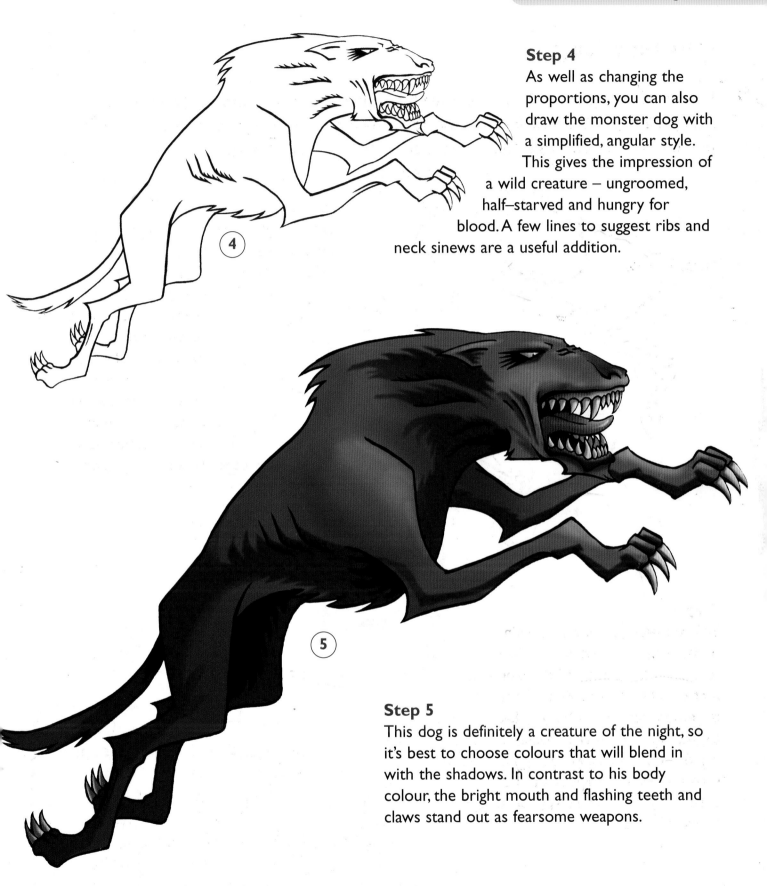

Step 4
As well as changing the proportions, you can also draw the monster dog with a simplified, angular style. This gives the impression of a wild creature – ungroomed, half–starved and hungry for blood. A few lines to suggest ribs and neck sinews are a useful addition.

Step 5
This dog is definitely a creature of the night, so it's best to choose colours that will blend in with the shadows. In contrast to his body colour, the bright mouth and flashing teeth and claws stand out as fearsome weapons.

More Skeletons

So far, we have been concentrating on mammals, but there are many more members of the animal kingdom that you might want to draw. Luckily, nearly all animals that live on land have the same parts to their skeletons, even though the proportions may be very different.

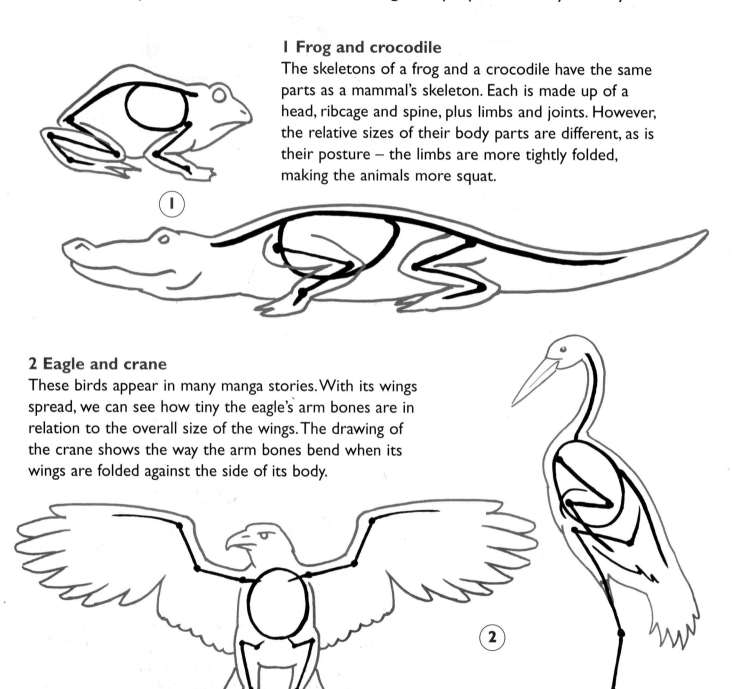

1 Frog and crocodile

The skeletons of a frog and a crocodile have the same parts as a mammal's skeleton. Each is made up of a head, ribcage and spine, plus limbs and joints. However, the relative sizes of their body parts are different, as is their posture – the limbs are more tightly folded, making the animals more squat.

2 Eagle and crane

These birds appear in many manga stories. With its wings spread, we can see how tiny the eagle's arm bones are in relation to the overall size of the wings. The drawing of the crane shows the way the arm bones bend when its wings are folded against the side of its body.

3 Dinosaur and crow

This dinosaur can stand fairly upright since its strong back legs can bear its weight. Over millions of years, birds have evolved from dinosaurs and still retain some of the same characteristics. The crow also stands on two legs. Its forelimbs are wings, but the overall bone structure is the same.

4 Wasp and spider

Wasps and spiders are invertebrates, so they have no spine. Like all insects, wasps have three main body segments and six legs. The legs are always attached to the middle body segment and the wings have no bones. Spiders have just two main body parts and an extra pair of legs.

Dinosaur – 3/4 View

This exercise shows how to draw a dinosaur in action from a 3/4 viewpoint.

Step 1
A large, roughly drawn circle forms the ribcage. Position and shape the skull, then add a curved line to this to mark the centre of the head. Add the parts of the spine and all the bones of the limbs.

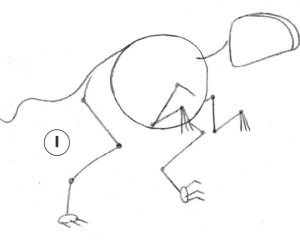

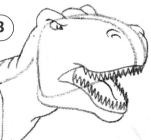

Step 2
Once you've completed the skeleton framework, use it to help you outline the flesh of the body. The claws on the forelimbs are curled under so that they are hidden. When you work on the head, copy the curves above the eyes. The mouth should be wide open, ready for you to add the teeth.

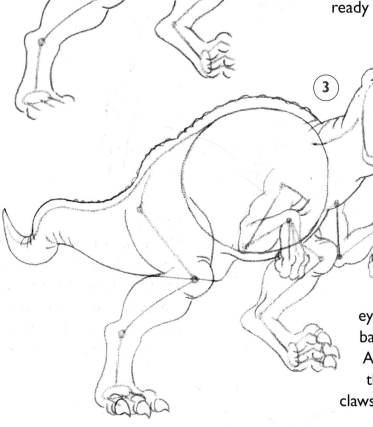

Step 3
Now fill the mouth with jagged teeth and draw the centre crease line of the tongue. Draw on the nostrils and the pupils of the eyes. Some tiny curves along the dinosaur's back will show the bumps of the spine. Adding crease lines to the body will show the folds of the thick skin. Put some sharp claws on the toes.

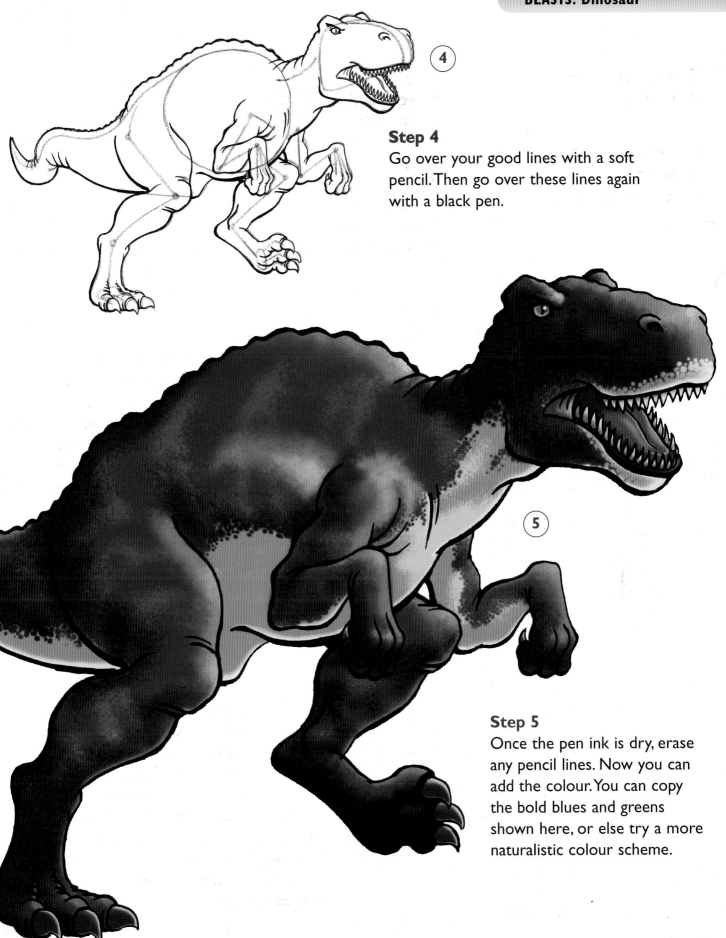

Step 4
Go over your good lines with a soft pencil. Then go over these lines again with a black pen.

Step 5
Once the pen ink is dry, erase any pencil lines. Now you can add the colour. You can copy the bold blues and greens shown here, or else try a more naturalistic colour scheme.

Glossary

anime The Japanese word for *animation*.

angular Having angles or sharp corners.

buckle Bend out of shape, warp or crumple.

distortion The bending or twisting of something out of its natural shape.

dynamic Full of energy.

framework Basic structure.

geometric Conforming to the laws of geometry, the study of the properties and relationships of points, lines, angles, curves, surfaces and solids.

highlight An area of very light tone in a painting that provides contrast or the appearance of illumination.

horizontal Parallel to the horizon.

joint Any of the parts of a body where bones are connected.

manga The literal translation of this word is "irresponsible pictures". Manga is a Japanese style of animation that has been popular since the 1960s.

muzzle The projecting part of an animal's face.

naturalistic Accurately imitating nature.

proportion The relationship between the parts of a whole figure.

stance The way someone or something stands.

stooge Comic sidekick.

stylized Aiming to achieve a particular effect, rather than a natural look.

symmetrical Describing an object in which the two halves are mirror images of each other.

texture The feel or appearance of a surface.

vertical Upright, or at a right angle to the horizon.

watercolour Paint made by mixing pigments (substances that give something its colour) with water.

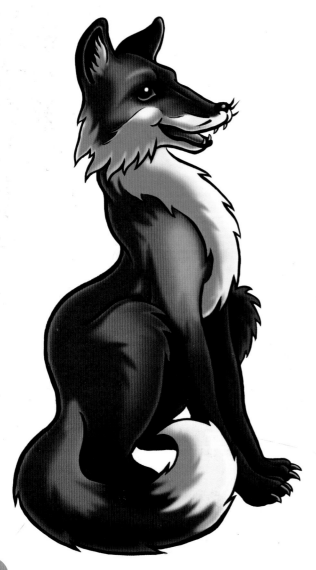

Further information

Books

The Art of Drawing Manga by Ben Krefta (Arcturus, 2003)

How to Draw Manga: A Step-by-Step Guide by Katy Coope (Scholastic, 2002)

How to Draw Manga: Compiling Characters (Volumes 1 & 2) by the Society for the Study of Manga Techniques (Japan Publications Trading Company, 2000)

Step-by-Step Manga by Ben Krefta (Scholastic, 2004)

Websites

http://www.polykarbon.com/
Click on "tutorials" for tips on all aspects of drawing manga.

http://omu.kuiki.net/class.shtml
The Online Manga University.

http://members.tripod.com/~incomming/
Rocket's How to Draw Manga.

Note to parents and teachers:

Every effort has been made by the publishers to ensure that these websites are suitable for children and contain no inappropriate or offensive material. However, because of the nature of the Internet, it is impossible to guarantee that the contents of these sites will not be altered. We strongly advise that Internet access is supervised by a responsible adult.

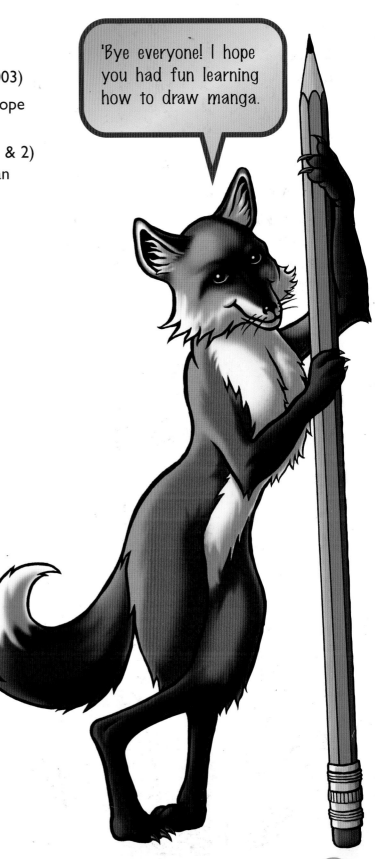

'Bye everyone! I hope you had fun learning how to draw manga.

Index